IoT Opportunities

All You Need to Know about the Internet of Things

Completely Updated to 2021!

by
Haylee Jackson

© 2021 Haylee Jackson

All rights reserved. This book or any portion thereof may not be reproduced or used in any manner without the written permission of the publisher except for the use of brief quotations in a book review.

Printed in the United States of America.

Website: www.iotopps.com

Disclaimer: This book is intended to provide general knowledge of the Internet of Things and is solely for educational purposes. Whilst the utmost care has been taken by the author there is no implied or express warranty as to accuracy and independent professional advice is recommended before acting on any of the content, with the express disclaimer of any liability howsoever arising.

Index

Index 3

About the IoT 6

What is IoT? 6

How is this Done? 6

The Core Point 8

What is the Future of the IoT? 10

Some Opening Opportunities 11

Inflection point 16

Coming Changes 20

What new opportunities will the IoT Drive?
.... 20

Where Changes are Happening 24

Automotive 28

Wearable Technology 34

Wearable Benefits 34

Wearable Capabilities 35

Applications of Wearables 36

What the Internet of Things means for your business 40

Business models 46

'The Internet of Things – A conceptual model' 46

5G and the IoT 47

IoT Open Innovation Challenges 50

Terms with which to become familiar 52

Resources and Acknowledgments 59

IoT Opportunities

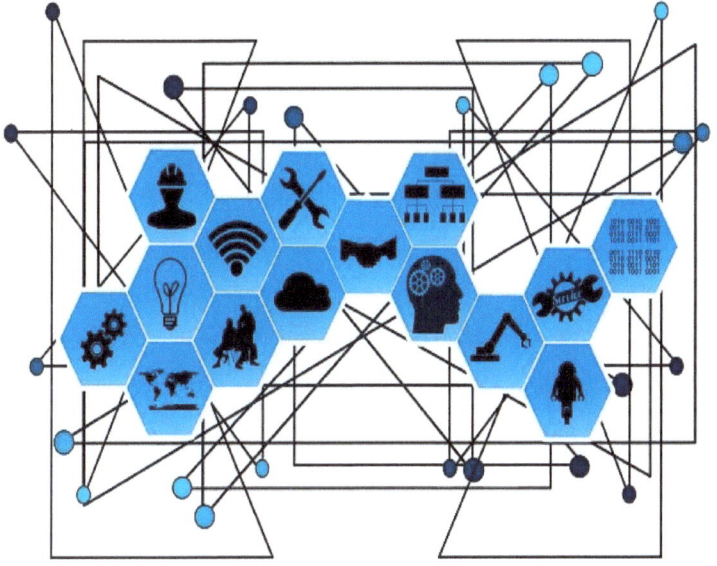

About the IoT

What is IoT?

IoT stands for the Internet of Things, namely the further development of the internet in which everyday objects have network connectivity allowing them to send and receive data. IoT innovation poses more of an opportunity, not a threat.

The IoT allows real-time data analytics and insights. It mainly harnesses the power of the cloud to run, store, and transmit data collected.

How is this Done?

Tiny embedded computers or microchips in the form of sensors and actuators fitted into objects, use hardware, software, and network connectivity that link these devices and record and share data. Currently, in 2020, there are about 50 billion connected devices worldwide. IoT devices capable of listening, learning, tracking, communicating, taking action and making predictions have become the norm.

Forecasts by these devices influence many aspects of our daily life, from traffic to room temperatures. Examples include real-time data allowing optimal traffic flows, getting police officers, fire engines or ambulances to scenes faster or even as small as recognizing when a room becomes occupied and turning on the heating or air conditioning.

The IoT is, can and continues to be incorporated into almost every aspect of our daily lives, not just smartphones and tablets. Objects, from cars, street lamps, traffic lights, bridges, to cash registers at stores, and so many more, are IoT-connected.

The applications of this technology are extensive, far-reaching and brimming with opportunities.

The Core Point

The primary objective is to apply this technology for collecting, analyzing, and using data as a resource in the business world. IoT data collected and analyzed on trends like spending and popular items amongst consumers is a valuable commodity. One core ability already available is to instantly plan a business model and products following where, how, when and what is trending with consumers.

For the IoT to accomplish these tasks, everyday objects become 'smart objects' by being connected with data collected and uploaded through the Internet. The data uploaded through these connections is then disbursed among legacy analytics backend-systems.

The analyzed data enables the user to make decisions about opportunities for efficiency gains, replacement or repair needs, or cost savings to benefit their business. IoT allows corporations to create working business models, revenue streams, and obtain information about markets.

IoT Opportunities

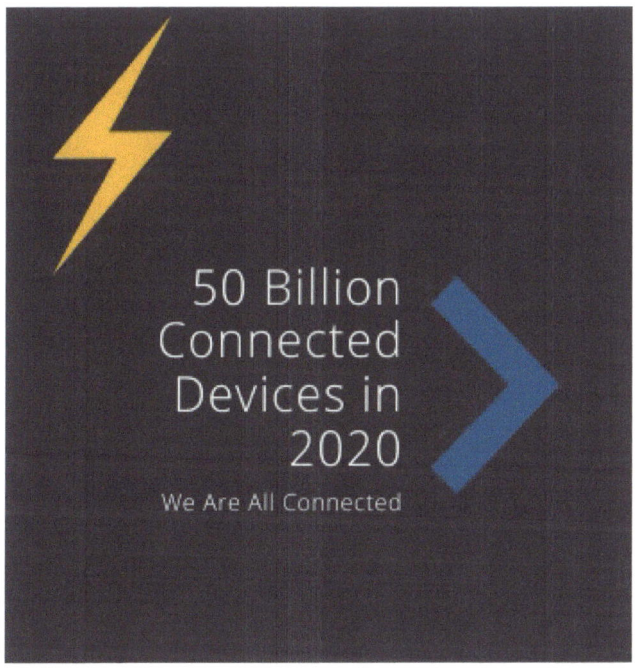

What is the Future of the IoT?

There have been multiple predictions about the IoT. One that came to pass is that there would be 50 billion IoT-connected objects or devices by 2020. This equates to roughly seven devices per person on Earth. McKinsey Global Institute estimates IoT impact will be as high as $6.2 trillion by 2025.

By then, the number of connected devices is expected to rise to 75 billion. It is forecast the U.S. will own 29% of global self-driving fleets by 2035. 54% of businesses cite cost-savings as their primary value-driver for IoT projects. Opportunities remain ripe for getting ahead and being a leader in IoT business models. You may be asking how to do I get in on this, or how will this help me?

Many multinational businesses are already on board. Alexa and Hey Google are ubiquitous in western homes. A plethora of online resources exists for you to sign up to the IoT. If you have not yet started, it is time to begin the shaping and development of your own business. The future is out there waiting for you.

The IoT can no longer be described as in its early – or even intermediate – stages. In 2020 it is entering its maturity phase.

Nevertheless, the gap remains open for you to grab the opportunity. Try out different plans or options, shape their usefulness, and harness the IoT to get ahead.

Some Opening Opportunities

The massively open and beckoning field of studies for IoT Developers can be broken down into:

- Devices;
- Resources;
- Controllers;
- Services;
- Databases;
- Web services;
- Analysis;
- Components; and,
- Applications.

With so many billions of dollars plunged into the IoT for development, research and implementation, there remains high demand for skilled mobile, chip, sensor, software,

IoT Opportunities

and app developers. Now is the very best time for new developers to climb aboard the IoT-wagon; then help grow and shape it.

Between the development and push for the IoT, the common complaint remains that progress is slower than anticipated.

This is down to the lack of skilled human resources. In these times of working from home, there has arguably never been a greater opportunity than upskilling yourself for the IoT.

The IoT is in the fast lane, and we should not underestimate the growth that will happen over the next year. Regardless of the size of your business, the IoT will work its way into this, if it has not already. Advance!

One of the foremost challenges facing the IoT in its earlier days was the number of different developer platforms. There was no standard available to developers. Fast-forward to 2021, however, and the toolsets plus developer support resources, have become far more defined and accessible.

IoT development is poised to accelerate. Among the most established developer platforms in 2021 are:

- Amazon Web Services (AWS)
- IBM Watson
- Microsoft Azure IoT

IoT Opportunities

- Google Cloud

These development platform systems enable developers to experience safe and secure as well as simple solution options for the IoT together with various other functions or objectives. The checklist includes data information analytics, network-connectivity, applications' development and enablement, automation, apart from IoT device plus data management and administration.

These platforms supply their clients risk-free and secure linking of numerous devices worldwide, no matter their physical locations. They enable smart city operations, power management, administration and monitoring, transport systems, industrial and commercial automation, among others.

An ongoing development area is in computer and online security.

A huge opportunity exists for developers to step up and create or enhance and refine secure, encrypted and private transfers that protect data and prevent hacking.

There are major drives for developers to get involved with the IoT and help create the advancements and improvements necessary to provide fully-functional operational data exchange.

Smart Cities are the future and will allow security, smart building, smart healthcare, smart energy, transportation, governance, smart homes, and smart infrastructure – these advances hold hugely beneficial outcomes provided they are done correctly.

This translates into a need for hardware and software developers who are adequately skilled. This primary IoT opportunity for developers is not only beneficial, but growing technological changes in computing and also manufacturing and renewable energy sources form part of the development of IoT.

Development of software to handle, exchange, and protect data, plus improve the objects and chips which make them 'smart' – such as household items ranging from lights, kitchenware, heating, TVs, and home networks, to robotics in factories and manufacturing – is ongoing.

Apart from mobile developers, major demand exists for people who can adapt chip designs and development processes for specific IoT system requirements.

The proliferation of IoT apps needs devices that are self-sustaining and operate on energy harvesting or long-life batteries. Semiconductor companies continue to address the constant need for minimal power consumption and optimal power management.

Connectivity-load is another critical concern, with hundreds or thousands of devices connected at the same time. The average smart home, for instance, contains up to 500 sensors connecting appliances, lights, thermostats and other devices, each with its low-power requirements.

Harnessing the power of the cloud and Wi-Fi is not enough for the IoT. As you can see, it is important to bring in more skilled developers for mobile and chip applications in smart objects.

Inflection point

With the advent of Alexa and Google Home, most of us are already familiar with how the IoT has permeated our everyday lives Consider when Bluetooth first appeared, not many people hopped aboard and there was not much interest. However, as companies began adopting and using it, a certain inflection point was reached where it became the must have, the new standard, something which we all know today.

Inflection point is an event resulting in significant change. You will no doubt agree that the inflection point of the IoT has already been reached.

According to McKinsey, the four critical indicators supporting the IoT are:

- Supplier attention

IoT developer tools and products have become increasingly available. Apple, for instance, offers HomeKit, HealthKit, CloudKit, SiriKit, DriverKit, ReplayKit, Camera and ARKit developer tools as part of its iOS operating-system upgrades. Google acquired Nest to catalyze its IoT development platform for smart home and other applications. The giant's smart home division is called Google Nest.

IoT Opportunities

- Technological advances

Semiconductor components integral to most IoT applications provide more functionality at ever-lower prices.

This tech capability leap is apparent in the growing market for smartphones and watches.

Although the declines of around 25 per cent year on year in the price of chip-sets could (naturally) not be sustained, increased automation and reduced staffing costs have kept this market strong.

- Increasing demand

Demand for second and third-generation IoT products (fitness bands, smartwatches and smart thermostats, for example) continues to increase as component technologies evolve and costs decline.

- Emerging standards

AI hardware is opening new opportunities for semiconductor companies. Many have joined forces with networking, hardware, and software companies.

In July 2020 Computer Weekly magazine wrote: "The oneM2M global campaign was established to give structure particularly to support IoT applications and service solutions that the majority of players in the

IoT arena position on their slide decks." OneM2M's practical design style is based upon an uncomplicated 3-layered model: application layer, typical service solutions layer, and network services solutions layer. This is practical| as the IoT is a merging (or maybe more precisely, the colliding of big established fields: IT; industrial/commercial systems, and also telecommunications.

These closely line up with the 3 layers of the oneM2M architecture. Namely, interoperability standards across industrial and general IoT environments to more reliably access and share data.

IoT Opportunities

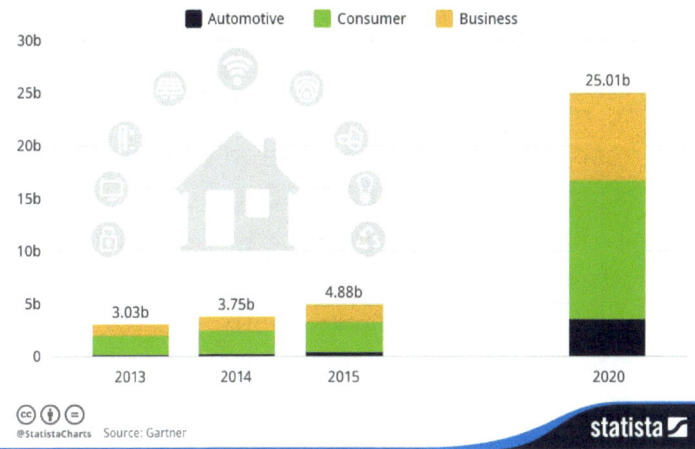

And it has...

Coming Changes

What new opportunities will the IoT Drive?

Change in Business Models

The IoT will force a major change in business models on many companies. It will help businesses create new value streams for customers, institute processes that speed time to market, triage market performance, and respond rapidly to customer needs. Fitness trackers like Fitbit Charge 2 and Garmin Vivosmart HR+ already aggregate data about our fitness habits and health stats and share these with strategic partners. There are plenty of organizations keen to get their hands on that kind of data for marketing and other purposes. The most important thing when considering how the IoT will affect your business is to think bigger — much bigger. It is not only about what products you can make 'smart,' or how information could affect your business efficiencies, or how you might sell that data to customers and associates.

The IoT has changed the playing field, and without exception, every business needs to consider and expand on its implications.

Real-time information:

A significant part of the IoT is not so much about smart devices as it is about sensors. These minute innovations attached to everything from yoghurt cups to the cement in bridges record and send data into the cloud. Analytics allow businesses to collect increasingly specific feedback on the use of a product or equipment when this breaks and even what users might want in the future. With the IoT, organizations capture data about their processes and products in a timely fashion for the creation of new revenue streams, improved operational efficiency and increased customer loyalty.

The need to dig deeper and provide well-informed recommendations based on real-time data is set to rise astronomically. At first, in-house staffers or consulting firms perform such services. Over time, however, business professionals well-versed in the specific skills required will handle these. Intelligent software is also increasingly performing this type of analysis for business-minded end-users.

Efficient, intelligent operations:

Once upon a time our phones were for making phone calls. Today, of course, consumers expect a lot more from the device they carry. Therefore, though strange or unnecessary at first glance to have a smart tennis racket (a Smart Tennis Sensor goes into the end of the racket and records data on every shot you play during a game or practice session), an IoT-enabled frying pan or a smart yoga mat, these are just some of the forays into the world of the IoT.

Smart grids already supply data to utility companies and allow organizations to make on-the-fly decisions concerning pricing, logistics, sales and support, deployment, and so forth.

Global visibility:

Rolls-Royce aircraft engines contain thousands of sensors that – after analysis in the cloud – send real-time engine function data to monitoring ground stations. These detect and warn of malfunctions before they become catastrophic, allow investigation of causes – plus, optimally, facilitate prevention – of aircraft disasters. Microsoft uses software to constantly collect data on what features are being used for their products, so they can strip away the least popular ones and focus on those most popular. The IoT makes it easier for enterprises to see across the business regardless of location, and improve tracking efficiency (without waste of time or money) and efficacy (the effectiveness or ability of something to produce the results you want) from one end of the supply chain to the other.

The IoT proficiently helps companies create new services and new revenue streams on top of traditional products, e.g., vending machine vendors offering inventory management to those who supply the goods stocked in the machine.

Where Changes are Happening

Retail

Retail operations have until now had relatively few functions fully connected. Sure, point of sales systems connected to inventory management systems and security systems have become intertwined with video, audio and sensory technology. Overall, this is mostly at the individual store level and provides little opportunity for retail franchises to manage productively. The 'Customer is King' and the King demands an excellent consumer experience; the IoT can play a central role in delivering it.

When customers call, retail agents will already know who they are, their purchase history and what they might want to buy next. The IoT allows for innovation, a lift in sales and a happier customer base.

One of the more recent trends is a particular concentration on an omnichannel strategy to increase client loyalty and retention via a seamless in-store experience. That includes supplying the client unchanged pricing, promotional deals plus personalized communication, multi-channel stock supply access, as well as other tailored client solutions. The objective being WiFi-linked facilities to aid consumers to achieve the most out of their shopping experience and encourage more personalized involvement with the seller.

Manufacturing

At any automobile manufacturing facility, there are hundreds if not thousands of tools connected to networks and storage devices, but more often than not, this information is kept in discrete computer silos.

The IoT delivers this information to a central intelligence forum, where it can then be used to quickly improve processes and achieve operational goals.

Medicine

Hospitals collect massive amounts of data. That information is now connected to central or aggregated intelligence-management structures, allowing deep, complex AI analysis and sharing.

Sure, hospital staff handles the distribution of drugs and monitoring of blood pressures. The IoT-data channeled into actions will dramatically improve care, reduce the length of hospital stays and lower the transmission of diseases and infection rates.

Automotive

Certain industries have so much information, innovation and interconnection to the IoT that Automotive gets its own chapter.

A forecast automotive IoT annual market worth over $540 billion by 2025 also supports this rationale.

Already, IoT-infused semi-autonomous vehicles make on-the-spot decisions and partially control vehicle operation to prevent accidents and lessen the responsibility-load on motorists. Together with various proximity sensor units and electronic cameras, vehicles are increasingly incorporating IoT systems to decrease human error and make driving ever more comfy and less risky.

Vehicles have become increasingly software-driven. The major IoT developments in the vehicle industry have been behind the scenes, with both vehicle manufacturers and software designers laying claim to the driver's seat.

A major U.S. player (and world influencer) when it comes to vehicle fleet management is AT&T. There is currently a proliferation of fleet management systems being used in the U.S. The "AT&T Drive" program seeks to unite the leading players in the automotive sector and together work towards the quickest tech advancements for the benefit of end-users.

AT&T has around 30 million connected in-service transportation devices in its IoT-related applications. It accounts for about 3 million fleet-managed vehicles in the U.S. and A&T is also the biggest private fleet owner in the U.S. with some 75,000 vehicles.

Approximately 90% of the top 10 fleet management providers in the U.S. market use connectivity services from AT&T.

Gartner estimates that in 2020, there are already 5.8 billion enterprise and automotive IoT endpoint applications.

All vehicles have become 'smart' vehicles. What do these smart vehicles do?

They use data more accurately and analytically. They integrate new data and maximize efficiencies, including predictive capabilities for performance, maintenance and operations.

The likely future scenario is the automotive management market dominated by a handful of providers with installed IoT bases. The IoT paired with Big Data within the auto industry, as illustrated by AT&T with its vast experience in the U.S. transport market, is fast becoming reality. The full portfolio of AT&T includes basic fleet- and asset-tracking plus more advanced solutions.

Vehicle fleets commonly use telematic systems from AT&T to improve management efficiency, proof of delivery, routes taken, and driver productivity. Its apps Tracking, and Reporting, operate smoothly and are well known. At least twenty-seven airlines, and also many shipping lines use AT&T's 'Cargo View' – monitoring and tracking over 300,000 containers globally.

The Automotive IoT holds a bright future for vehicles, including driverless cars, buses and taxis, the tracking of shipments, locations of planes, ships, cargo, air and road freight, fleets, and providing navigation and vehicle upkeep to ensure safety.

As electric autonomous vehicles become more common, applying the IoT to fleets and individual vehicles will decrease the number of Department of Transportation violations and motor accidents, and should save significantly on insurance costs. The IoT also provides cost-effective software updates to vehicles resulting in time and money savings.

Fully autonomous vehicles, capable of driverless operation and safe travel, have already become a worldwide reality.

In terms of business opportunity, automotive is one of the best fields, wide open to you or your business. The IoT will continue to disrupt and provide explosive growth in the automotive industry, particularly with autonomous vehicles. Of course, vehicles do not just include cars, buses, trucks, and airplanes, but marine vehicles too.

IoT Opportunities

IoT Opportunities

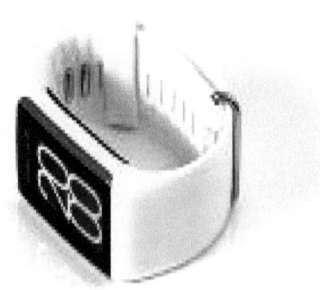

Wearable Technology

Wearables are the next major achievement in cognitive computing. Concentric circles of connected networks encompass Wearables and the IoT

- Smart Body – Body area network
- Smart Life – Personal area network (home, car, work)
- Smart World – Wireless sensor network (streets, buildings, places).

Wearable Benefits

Hands-free, allowing the wearer to multi-task.

Continuous, consistent interaction with the body.

Immediate access to information.

Frictionless authentication.

Suited to the wearer's context.

IoT wearables already play an ever-increasing role in monitoring one's body, immediately being able to search and find information without needing a smartphone or computer, removing some time-consuming steps looking up information and data, keeping track of where you are to prevent getting lost, have directions on hand, and so much more.

Wearable Capabilities

Sensory integration. Augmented, virtual and mixed reality. Communication and media. Wearables as controllers. Medical aids.

As futuristic as they may sound, wearable options already improve many persons' physical abilities such as hearing and vision, help convert texts into audible playbacks for the sight-impaired and help guide them. The IoT is creating a far more immersive world through better hands-free options for pictures, videos, even creating hands-free controls for television, radios and more.

Under 'Smart Life' or personal area networks (PANs), wearables interact with computers, tablets, smartphones and IoT in your home, car and work, to monitor, communicate and automate.

Applications of Wearables

Controllers. Wearable devices control your car, home and office equipment, enterprise apps and systems.

Optimization. Wearable data optimizes worker productivity or the temperature in your home.

Automation. Wearables comprehend and interpret your needs and then automatically handle tasks.

Risk mitigation. Wearable technology saves lives, deters crime, and reduces human error.

Communication. How do/will wearables play a pivotal role in centralizing all your communication needs in your home, car and office?

IoT Opportunities

What should you do?

Firstly, with the vast array of opportunities out there, you need to decide which one suits you best.

Ask yourself: what are my / my business's core competencies?

Where does my business excel in comparison with competitors? What is my USP? The intersection of market opportunities and core competencies forms the basis of launching new products and services.

Idea generation may be described as a constrained optimization challenge.

Combining core competencies in different ways and matching them to market opportunities, you or your business can launch compelling new products and services.

The Intelligence Age is delivering enhanced experiences that turn the mundane into the remarkable. These moments present opportunities to develop new products and services that, from 2021, will create the next economic boom in America and worldwide. Its momentum has even been accelerated by the COVID-19 saga of 2020/21.

IoT Opportunities

What the Internet of Things means for your business

As robotics increasingly dominate, the need for routine work carried out by people will continue to decrease. Amazon, for example is expanding the automation of its barcoded product selection and packaging, with drone shipping of purchases already a reality. Working from home has become the new buzz phrase. But, for people working in shops and offices, there will always be tasks requiring creativity and problem-solving skills. Robots are incapable of empathy, which only people can provide. People have to determine their human capabilities and develop new skills that, for example, may relate to the programming or maintenance and repair of robots. What do you need to do for your business plan? Well, here is a start:

Develop a cloud plan

'Cloud' technology fits right in with the IoT. When we realize worldwide integration is the future of business, we can begin to prepare for it. Among your chief concerns in this area is how your business satisfies and fulfils the demands of customers, clients and employees, who now expect complete transparency and connectivity.

In a cloud computing system, there is a significant workload shift. Local computers no longer have to do all the heavy lifting in running software applications. The network of computer servers that makes up the cloud handles them instead. Hardware and software demands on the user's side decrease. The only thing the user's computer needs to be able to run is the cloud computing system interface, via a web browser such as Chrome or Internet Explorer, and the cloud network takes care of the rest.

Replace old technology

Although we might even prefer the machinery, equipment, and technology we have used for the past decade, we are going to need a good spring-cleaning eventually.

Once the IoT wave kicks into high gear, companies lacking the technology to take advantage of a total Internet revolution will be left in the dust. Not only will the number of devices using the Internet increase, but the digital and physical worlds will become one. Already, thanks to the IoT, there are rides shared on taxi-services Uber (current market capitalization around $80 billion) and Lyft, and houses let through Airbnb. The IoT will not only positively affect tech-industries but all businesses. When upgrading existing technology, make sure your new gear can be fully integrated with all aspects of your business.

Increase capacity management

According to Raritan, a leader in data center infrastructure management, when the IoT transformation is complete, 'data centers will be faced with an overwhelming amount of data that will need to be synthesized, analyzed, and stored.' To prepare for this, data center operators must determine existing levels of network capacity and how to use that storage space better. Those who collect, analyze, manage and handle this data in a meaningful way, who can use big data, provide solutions to market challenges, and foster understanding of new complex systems, will hold power in the future.

Become network-ubiquitous

Everything that plugs into an electrical outlet should be designed to connect to the

Internet. This includes phones, printers, manufacturing machinery, security systems, lights, blinds, aircons and more. Whenever you encounter new technology with IoT-network connectivity features, go for it.

Tackle security issues

Experts predict network security will become one of the most important aspects of business, which makes sense since security is the underbelly of total connectivity.

Investing in high-quality data security solutions that are scalable and robust can only help your business. News stories daily hit the headlines about systems being hacked and corrupted, private data is stolen, even ransoms are demanded and paid against the threat of destruction of data files. Encryption specialists have a bright future indeed. There is no leeway when it comes to the security of your IoT products or devices.

Invest in education

A two-step process: First, your business needs to spend time educating existing employees on the IoT shift, and how it affects their roles in the firm; Second, your recruitment and hiring processes need adapting to locate talent having a firm grasp of new technology and coming developments. Renewable energy is set to harvest sunlight, wind and water motion and recycling of waste (including human waste), without any external sources of energy. This will revolutionize the energy market – which alone forms ten percent of the global economy. It may be wise to educate yourself and invest in these renewable and green energy sources and developments.

Market your progressiveness

The latest generation of consumers was entirely raised on the Internet. They appreciate and understand the IoT regarding its design and function, and social media.

Empathy, Neurochemistry, and the Dramatic Arc – concerning data gathering – are also research subjects worth studying. Current business models are battling to keep up with strides in the digital world when it comes to products, sales and marketing. Once your business has reached the point where it can really say it is a full participant in this change, do not be afraid to tout this.

IoT Opportunities

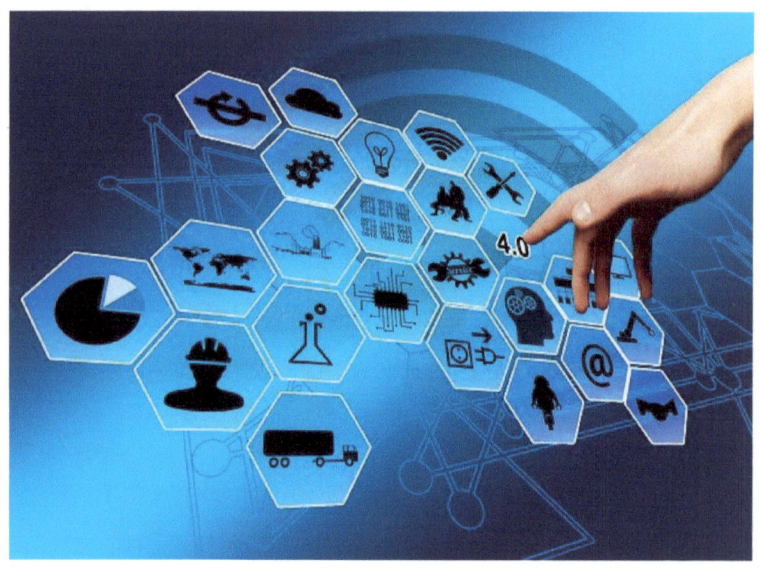

Business models

'The Internet of Things – A conceptual model'

Businesses based on intellectual property (IP) are no longer new. During its ascent, Microsoft created much of today's infrastructure for software patents, (thanks to a certain Mr Gates Sr. in the legal department).

The Open-Source IoT provides clear opportunities in two areas.

The first is in providing new hardware for sensors, actuators, gateways and data centers plus the required hardware connectivity in sensor nets and public infrastructure.

The second is in providing services that add value based on the rich connectivity afforded by an open infrastructure. The best business models will be those that take advantage of connectivity and standards, rather than the ones that create vertical silos, walled gardens, and lock-ins, regardless of exclusivity of the Intellectual Property. Besides, recent legal battles have illustrated the futility of pretending to own something everyone uses or does anyway.

5G and the IoT

The IoT will gain a great deal of advancement with the implementation of 5G. Bear in mind that prior to 4G, the steaming of movies on Netflix, Amazon Prime and the like, was stop-start at best. 5G is simply the next step in the progression of networks of sensors and software applications to provide practically any capability to send out and get information. A 5G network will sustain over 2 million linked sensors per square mile.

Undoubtedly, modern IoT tech and innovation is becoming so ubiquitous that any kind of advantages for the IoT equate to pluses for almost every other sector.

Noteworthy applications include the consumer IoT gadget market with virtual conversations (such as Alexa and Hey Google), and once these smart devices take advantage of the 5G framework, consumers will certainly find them even more interesting and appealing. Adjusting the heating even when the Wi-Fi has crashed, for instance; the enhanced dependability as well as unbelievable speed of 5G driving smart home gizmos will almost certainly become vital when it comes to safety and security protection tools such as like video cameras and also smart locks. If there is an unlawful intrusion, a fire, or flooding in the basement, the quickest possible reaction is clearly wanted – and sensors, data processors and AI driven by 5G will be the ultimate answer.

Other opportunities will arise for IoT in the home entertainment market as the capacity of 5G to move enormous quantities information with such reduced latency, that ultra-immersive virtual and augmented virtual reality (AR/VR) and video gaming experiences beyond anything imagined to date, will become possible – having the processing power in the cloud, no noticeable lag, those annoyingly bulky headsets will fade into distant memory.

The IoT will additionally utilize the power of 5G networks to "slice" numerous digital networks on the very same system. This also implies a distinctive network might be allocated solely to security-based IoT tools so their uptime is prioritized over less important service solutions.

Steve Szabo, vice president of IoT at Verizon Business, claims: 'The potential of 5G to transform business operations is immense, enabling use-cases that don't exist today.' In regard to the opportunities 5G will enable, he referred to near real-time simulation, evaluation, analysis, and forecasts through AI plus machine-learning and revision, as only a few of the applications that low-latency IoT transmission will make possible in every sector – from smart homes to self-driven vehicles to robotics to wearables.

5G will enhance avoidance of human error and take over complex tasks of autonomous systems, like commercial vehicle self-driving operations, with multiple data feedback on routes, performance, and safety.

One obstacle in the UK, for example, according to communications regulator Ofcom's Connected Nations 2019 report, is 4G coverage on only about 62 percent of motorways and 46 percent of B roads, so travel safety can only improve as these networks expand.

The automotive industry will accelerate connectivity. Increasing numbers of sensors and cameras monitoring from traffic signals to water pipes, and cities connecting with each other, will enable smart vehicles to tap into this data for real-time feedback for safe efficient road trips.

In manufacturing, 5G will be far cheaper than wired networks, and be able to achieve so much more, with less latency, hugely improved communication speed and resultant cost benefits lower accident rates. Systems will update near-instantly at around 1ms, compared to 25ms with 4G connections. Companies which embrace 5G, more so in tandem with AI, will instantly get the precise data to the exact place needed, and quickly outpace their competitors. The same applies to AR and VR applications, which will increasingly play a role in instant problem-solving, in many spheres, from surgery to creating overlays of component replacement in manufacturing.

IoT Open Innovation Challenges

There are many IoT Open Innovation challenges nowadays and if you are an innovator you will easily find these online.

Constantly, new models of innovation merge the differentiation between colleges, businesses and governments, and even communities. They use disruptive innovation and modern technology such as the cloud, the IoT plus Big Data, to address and resolve social difficulties, sustainably, profitably, quicker as well as more capably than in the past.

IoT Opportunities

IoT Jargon

Terms with which to become familiar

It is good to familiarize yourself with any general terms and some IoT jargon you do not already know.

Open platform for Developers – IoT app developers are needed to provide and put together high-level services and data sources in such a way that users can easily manage them. There is a need to build into IoT platforms standard, frictionless, transparent mechanisms for user authentication and provenance along with commands and data.

Open participation for Users – IoT users participate in creating their applications and managing their information in ways not previously possible. The role of a user as the composer of IoT application graphs gives the user an agency in customizing their own experience. At the same time, it requires a new level of composability in services and data sources.

IoT Device- ITU-T Y.2060 – A piece of equipment with the mandatory capabilities of communication and the optional capabilities of sensing, actuation, data capture, data storage and data processing.

WoT Device- SWOT model – WoT device is a 'Thing' with enabled WoT connectivity. A 'Thing' in the Web of Things (WoT) can be any object that has a unique identifier and which can send/receive web resources (including information and data) over a network.

Constrained Devices- IETF RFC 7228 – Small devices with limited CPU, memory, and power resources, so-called 'constrained' devices. Constrained devices might be in charge of gathering information in diverse settings, including natural ecosystems, buildings, and factories, and sending the information to one or more server stations. They might also act on information, by performing some physical action, including displaying it.

Constrained devices may work under severe resource constraints such as limited battery and computing power, little memory, and insufficient wireless bandwidth and ability to communicate; these constraints often exacerbate each other and provide a challenge and opportunity to overcome them.

Web Server- A web server stores, processes and delivers web pages to clients. The communication between client and server takes place using the Hypertext Transfer Protocol (HTTP). Pages delivered are most frequently HTML documents, which may include images, style sheets and scripts in addition to text content.

Sensors - devices that measure physical quantities or qualities and convert them into digital signals, read by observers or instruments.

User-agent – A type of Web agent or piece of software acting on behalf of a person.

Standards Body – Standards Bodies are responsible for the common-use specifications of a platform or system of platforms.

They are usually composed of representatives from corporations and public institutions, and experts in the field. An open standards process allows equitable participation of any qualified person, without any licensing restrictions, regardless of institutional affiliation or lack of them.

IoT Opportunities

Open-Source Software – generally recognized as software available in human-readable and maintainable source code form, to any developer who follows the provisions of the license. Open-source software has both its copyright and license usually free. The word 'copyleft' is sometimes used to describe open-source license terms.

Open-Source hardware – The basic idea is the same as Open-Source software, in that the design specifications, schematics, board layout, and firmware are available for anyone 'skilled in the art' to reproduce the hardware for any purpose as long as the terms of the license are followed.

Open API – An Application Programming Interface allows developers to build applications on a platform or to communicate with other applications and services. The idea of an API is to open the system at a particular point to allow developers to build onto the system without signing a license or NDA. This gives the platform provider control over how developers can use the platform, while allowing anyone to develop on, and add value to, the platform.

IoT Opportunities

'Double-smart' data is transmitted based on thresholds or internal logic of sensors measuring this.

'Triple-smart' data is processed 'on-site' and includes analysis and conclusions being transmitted by sensors.

Low energy wireless IP networks – embedded radio in system-on-a-chip designs, lower power Wi-Fi, sub-GHz radio in an ISM band, often using a compressed version of IPv6 called 6LowPAN.

ZigBee – communication technology based on the IEEE 802.15.4 2.4 GHz-band radio protocol to implement physical and MAC layer for low-rate wireless Private Area Networks. Some of its main characteristics such as low power consumption, low data rate, low cost, and high message throughput make it an interesting IoT enabler technology.

Z-Wave – a communication protocol that is mostly used in smart home applications. It uses a radio protocol in the 900 MHz-band.

Thread – Like ZigBee, this IoT communication technology relies on the IEEE 802.15.4 2.4 GHz-band radio protocol. A key difference is that its networking protocol is IPv6-compatible.

LTE-Advanced – LTE-A is a high-speed communication specification for mobile networks. Compared to its original LTE, LTE-A has been improved to have extended coverage, higher throughput and lower latency.

One important application of this technology is Vehicle-to-Vehicle (V2V) communications.

Wi-Fi-Direct – Essentially Wi-Fi is for peer-to-peer communication without needing to have an access point. This feature attracts IoT apps to be built on top of Wi-Fi-Direct to benefit from the speed of Wi-Fi while they experience lower latency (or "lagging").

HomePlug – This networking standard used to enable IoT communication over a home or building's power lines.

MoCA – A networking standard to enable IoT communication over CATV-type coaxial cable.

Ethernet – A general-purpose networking standard used to enable IoT communication over twisted pair or fiber network links.

Hacker jargon 'pwn' (pawn) – 'Own' (as in take over), or 'take control of' or 'hack'.

Thank you for reading my book which I hope has helped provide you a basic overview of the Internet of Things and how it can influence your life and future business opportunities.

Your positive review of this book would be most appreciated.

It's quick and easy.

Resources and Acknowledgments

This book has been written with acknowledgment to the following sources, and includes those directly quoted or accessible within the body of the book. No copyright infringement is intended; should you feel there has been any such infringement, please email the author on davidpmeister@gmail.com so that your concerns may be addressed.

http://www.McKinsey.com

http://www.business.att.com/enterprise/Portfolio/internet-of-things/ http://iofthings.org

Bauer, Harald, Mark Patel, and Jan Veira. 'The Internet of Things: Sizing up the Opportunity.' *Mckinsey*. <http://www.mckinsey.com/industries/high-tech/our-insights/the-internet-of-things-sizing-up-the-opportunity>.

Marr, Bernard. '3 Ways the IoT Will Change Every Business.' Chase. <https://www.chase.com/commercial-bank/executive-connect/nc20-3-ways-iot>.

Schmarzo, Bill. '5 Ways the Internet of Things Drives New $$$ Opportunities.' *Infocus.emc.com*. N.p.

<https://infocus.emc.com/william_schmarzo/5-ways-the-internet-of-things-drives-new-opportunities/>.

Pickett, Dan. 'What the 'Internet of Things' Means for Enterprising Entrepreneurs.' *Entrepreneur*. N.p. <http://www.entrepreneur.com/article/239782>.

Att.com. <http://resources.att.com/what-you-need-to-know-about-iot>.

AMYX, AUTHOR: SCOTT AMYX, AMYX+MCKINSEY. SCOTT. 'How to Create the Next Billion Dollar Opportunity in Wearables, Internet of Things.' *Wired*. Amyx+McKinsey<http://www.wired.com/insights/2014/08/create-next-billion-dollar-opportunity-wearables-internet-things/>.

Mikkonen, Johannes. '5 Ways the Internet of Things Will Change Your Business.' *Http://www.demoshelsinki.fi/*. <http://www.demoshelsinki.fi/en/2015/12/07/5-ways-the-internet-of-things-will-change-your-business/>.

Rampton, John. 'How Will the Internet of Things Affect Your Business?'*Forbes*. <http://www.forbes.com/sites/johnrampton/how-will-the-internet-of-things-affect-your-business/#691c93f54421>.

Koster, Michael. 'Data Models for the Internet of Things.' *Ot-datamodels*. N.p. <http://iot-datamodels.blogspot.com/12/the-internet-of-things-needs-open.html>.

<http://www.w3.org/WoT/IG/wiki/Terminology>.

https://www.computerweekly.com/opinion/Is-data-interoperability-the-key-to-unlocking-IoT-value

https://www.amazon.com/IoT-Opportunities-about-Internet-Things-ebook/dp/B01M31PI3V

www.ingramcontent.com/pod-product-compliance
Lightning Source LLC
Chambersburg PA
CBHW041107180526
45172CB00001B/143